Anxiety Be Gone

A journal to relax, reset,
and move forward

PETER PAUPER PRESS, INC.
WHITE PLAINS, NEW YORK

PETER PAUPER PRESS
Fine Books and Gifts Since 1928

OUR COMPANY

In 1928, at the age of twenty-two, Peter Beilenson began printing books on a small press in the basement of his parents' home in Larchmont, New York. Peter—and later, his wife, Edna—sought to create fine books that sold at "prices even a pauper could afford."

Today, still family owned and operated, Peter Pauper Press continues to honor our founders' legacy—and our customers' expectations—of beauty, quality, and value.

Illustrations used under license from Shutterstock.com
Additional illustrations by David Cole Wheeler
Designed by Heather Zschock

Visit us at www.peterpauper.com

Hello, and thanks for joining!

If you're reading this, you're ready to seriously banish your anxiety. (If your anxiety is reading this: Get lost! This book isn't for you!)

Anxiety isn't just super annoying. It's also always there. It's so present, it can be hard to know who you are without it. And it's so powerful that it can take a huge toll on your self-esteem. But you're a cool freaking person, and there's so much more to you than your fears. This book can't cure your anxiety, but it can give you a much-needed break, a better understanding of anxiety's sneaky tricks, and a glimpse of yourself beyond the shadow fear casts. Consider this journal a tool in your anti-stress arsenal. It's designed to help you let go of the past, look forward to the future, and enjoy the moment (all things anxiety hates, that mood-killer).

The pages ahead will distract you from stress and help you deal with anxiety in a healthy way, forgive yourself, and build yourself up. If your anxiety is telling you there's a perfect way to complete this journal, it's wrong! There are NO rules here, and there is no wrong or right way to enjoy this book. You can complete the activities chronologically, or skip around and do whatever feels right. When you're feeling stressed, crack this book open and say: "Anxiety, be gone!"

Stress Bubbles

Remember blowing soap bubbles as a kid, and how the bubbles filled the air around you? Anxiety is like that, but way less cute. Because stress is everywhere, it can be hard to track down its sources. Figuring out where your anxieties come from can help you pop the bubbles of stress as fast as life can blow them.

Fill each bubble with something that's giving you grief. Then, below each stressor, write one thing you can do to lessen your anxiety and pop that bubble!

Anxiety Monster

Anxiety is something you have, but it's not who you are. Imagine it's a monster hiding under your bed, and pull out a flashlight to see what you're dealing with. By looking your anxiety monster in the eye, you can begin to reject the scary stories it feeds you. So tell us about your little monster!

What's your anxiety monster's name?

_____

What does _____ look like?

_____

_____

_____

_____

What does _____ do to bother you?

_____

_____

_____

_____

What do you think _____ wants from you?

_____

_____

_____

_____

Draw or collage your anxiety monster:

About Me

People like to say "think positively" or "be confident." But it can be hard to know where to begin, especially if you've spent a lot of your life being hard on yourself, so here's a guide to help you get started. Don't be shy!

Something that makes me happy is

....

....

People usually compliment me on

....

....

I'm proud of myself when I

....

....

I'm funniest when

....

....

I practice kindness through

....

....

I support my friends by

....

....

People know I love them when

....

....

It's only your opinion that matters in your life and in your self-love and your self-worth.

BILLIE EILISH

What Pushes Your Panic Button?

Figuring out your triggers can make it harder for anxiety to ambush you. Some people get short of breath when they have to make a phone call. (Thanks, anxiety, that's so helpful.) The energy rush of coffee can send others into freak-out mode, or insomnia can make everything seem terrifying. Your anxiety's Kryptonite may be crowds, money, or a whole bunch of completely different stuff.

Rate the common triggers on the following pages from **0** (completely chill) to **10** (slams the big red panic button in your brain). Then note a few of your own specific triggers. Anxiety is easier to live with when you take the mystery out of it.

10 PANIC!

9 really terrible

8 terrible

7 very stressful

6 pretty stressful

5 kind of stressful

4 okay-ish

3 okay

2 almost chill

1 mostly chill

0 completely chill

TRIGGER	Anxiety level (0-10)
Crowds	
Meeting new people	
Conflict with a stranger	
Conflict with someone I know	
Being alone	
Public speaking	
Tests and exams	
Writing emails or letters	
Talking on the phone	
Social media	
Meetings	
Going somewhere new	
Going outside	
Schedule changes	
Rushing	
Long-term projects	
Big life changes	
Talking about emotions	
Germs	

Driving or being in a car	
Taking public transit	
Bugs	
Rodents	
Other animal(s) that freak you out:	
Making mistakes	
Not being liked	
Not fitting in socially	
Embarrassment	
Going to the doctor	
Money issues	
Caffeine	
Alcohol and other substances	
Sleep issues	
Other:	

Do what you can, with what you've got, where you are.

BILL WIDENER

Anxiety Bucket List

Bucket lists aren't only for once-in-a-lifetime stunts like climbing Mount Kilimanjaro or zip lining through a rainforest. They can also help you tackle smaller-scale (though no less heart-pounding) ventures like taking a new class or eating out alone. List some things that make you anxious, but that you want to do anyway. Then cross them out one by one as you do them!

1)

2)

3)

4)

5)

6)

7)

8)

9)

10)

"I haven't been everywhere,
but it's on my list.
SUSAN SONTAG

Collaging Core Values

Because stress is often so all-consuming, it can obscure what matters most to you. But you deserve a chance to focus on your role in this world, without anxiety bugging you for attention.

Take a minute to reflect on your core values.

What issues do you care about?

....

....

....

....

....

....

How do you believe people should treat one another?

....

....

....

....

....

....

....

....

How do you put your principles into practice?
How would you like to do so in the future?

*When we contemplate the whole globe as one great **dewdrop** . . . the whole universe appears as an infinite storm of **beauty.***

JOHN MUIR

A kind act can sometimes be as powerful as a sword.

RICK RIORDAN

A Friend to Call

Who helped you out at a time when you were totally stressed?

....

....

....

What did they do?

....

....

....

....

....

....

How can you put that energy out into the world?

....

....

....

....

....

....

Now, give that friend a call! Seriously!

Heavy Lifting

Even bodybuilders can't lift everything all the time. They take rest days, smoothie breaks, and even remove some weights when they need it! What are six things weighing you down?

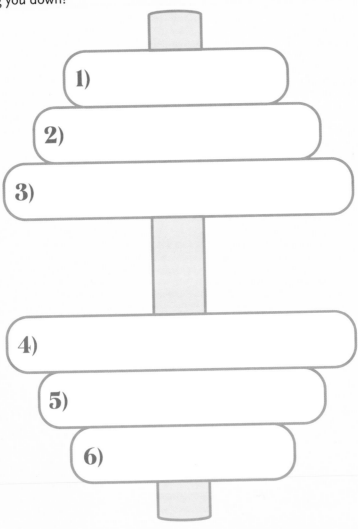

1)

2)

3)

4)

5)

6)

Circle the ones you can let go of, then whip up the ultimate smoothie to recharge the athlete in you, and color it in!

Smoothie ingredients:

- [ ] Milk
- [ ] Yogurt
- [ ] Agave nectar
- [ ] Honey
- [ ] Apples
- [ ] Kiwis
- [ ] Bananas
- [ ] Chocolate
- [ ] Peanut butter
- [ ] Spinach
- [ ] Blueberries
- [ ] Strawberries
- [ ] Mint
- [ ] Avocado
- [ ] ....
- [ ] ....
- [ ] ....

Masks

Masks are worn for performance, disguise, and protection. A mask tells one story, and conceals another. We all wear masks in our lives to share and obscure different aspects of ourselves. A mask might showcase style and courtesy, but hide anxieties and a sense of humor. By keeping parts of ourselves private, masks can make us feel safe, but they can also prevent us from truly being known by others.

*Using drawings, symbols, and words, fill in this mask
with the ways other people see you.*

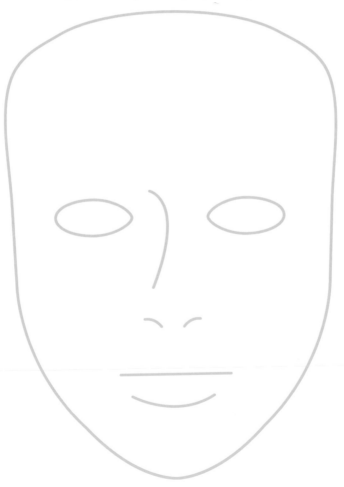

What are three aspects of yourself that your mask conceals?

1) ....

2) ....

3) ....

Why do you conceal these aspects?

How could you bring one of these traits to the surface and reveal some of what's behind that mask?

Flower Power

Let's gather some gratitude! Fill this flower's petals with the people and things you're thankful for.

Why are you thankful for these things?

How will you keep this flower with you?

How can you grow a garden with your gratitude?

Wise Mind

Contrary to popular belief, the answer to anxiety isn't logic, it's wisdom. When anxiety tells you, "don't go to that party, everyone hates you," logic replies, "everyone doesn't hate you; most people at that party don't even know you." It's only wisdom that says, "you can't control people's perceptions of you, but you deserve to have a good time anyway."

What's some nonsense anxiety is telling you?

....

....

....

How would logic respond?

....

....

....

What would wisdom say?

....

....

....

Another way of thinking about this is to consider three states of mind: the **Emotional Mind**, which is ruled by feelings; the **Rational Mind**, which is ruled by facts; and the **Wise Mind**, which both respects your feelings and responds rationally.

In the Venn diagram below, jot down experiences you've had with each of your three minds.

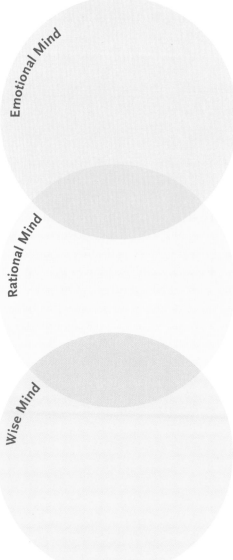

Draw it Out!

It's time to draw! For this exercise, take out two different colored markers (or pencils, or crayons). Consider **anger**. Close your eyes and ask: If this feeling had a shape, form, weight, temperature, texture, what would it look like? Using one of the markers, draw that below, using shapes and lines. When you're done, take the second marker, and do the same for **peace**—you can do this right on top of your last drawing. Think about how these two feelings look together.

Choose two new colors. With one, draw JOY.
Then with the other, draw SADNESS.

Again, choose two new colors.
Now draw ANXIETY, and then on top, draw CALM.

*One more! Take out two more colors, and with one,
draw FEAR. Then with the other, draw EXCITEMENT.*

Healing is a matter of time, but it is sometimes
also a matter of opportunity.

HIPPOCRATES

Extremely Chill Vacation

Pack your bags! You're going on vacation from anxiety. (Yes, you.) Destination: A place where there's nothing you need to worry about, nothing you need to do, and you're completely safe. Kick back and enjoy your luxurious, all-expenses-paid trip to a beach house, a French castle, the moon, or wherever else you want to go.

Where are you going?

....

....

Where will you stay, and what does your room look like? (A cottage? A hotel room with a view? A space station?)

....

....

....

....

What will you do? (Walk by the sea? Crafts? Hang out in your room?)

....

....

What are the meals like?

....

....

What are you looking forward to most?

....

....

....

Send a postcard home! Draw your anxiety-free destination on the front of the card, and write a message on the back.

Best Friend Contract

Name three people who have been good friends to you:

1) ....

2) ....

3) ....

What makes them good friends?

....

....

....

....

How are you a good friend in return?

....

....

....

....

The only way to have a friend is to be one.

RALPH WALDO EMERSON

It's time to add a fourth person to that list: you! So often, we are our own worst enemies, but we don't have to be! Just like you're a great friend to those you care about, you can be a great friend to yourself as well. So fill out this contract and start having a best friend on call 24/7.

The Best Friend Contract

I promise to be

_____

I will not judge myself for

_____

When I mess up, I will

_____

I will make myself laugh by

_____

When I need support, I will

_____

Signed:

Just DO It!

"Yeah, yeah," you're probably saying, "it's not that easy." And you're right—doing things, especially important things, can be really hard. Tasks can cause a lot of anxiety, and often there's internal pressure to do them perfectly. Even something as small as an email to your boss can seem impossible. Your head is full of worries: Is the email polite? Is it necessary? Is anything misspelled? Does it sound desperate? These questions overrun your brain, giving you no peace, so you put off the task. But the more you put it off, the harder it gets to complete!

Take a breath. While you can't answer all of the questions that plague you, you can make it a little easier to finish the job. Let's break it up!

Pick a task, big or small, and break it into manageable chunks. Here's an example:

Task (awful): Email boss about new project

Task (in cute little pieces):
- Write email header
- Say hello and good morning
- Summarize project (2 sentences)
- Ask question
- Spell check and send!

Now you try! Pro tip: If the pieces still feel impossible, break them down even further! Each piece should seem almost too easy. Don't forget to check each one off as you complete them!

Task (awful):

Task (in cute little pieces):

1)

2)

3)

4)

5)

Morning Routine

How you start the day influences your state of mind. A good morning routine sets you up to be more productive, creative, and most importantly, more calm.

What do you normally do each morning?

....

....

....

How long does it take you to get ready?

....

What do you eat for breakfast? Is it enough fuel to start your day, or do you get hungry again in an hour?

....

....

What small thing(s) could you do to make your morning a better start to your day? (Add something soothing to your routine? Do something the night before, so you're not rushing?)

....

....

....

Write some words of encouragement you can say to yourself in the mirror every morning to start the day right:

....

....

Wake up tomorrow and say it!

Now draw some latte art in the coffee cup, and wish yourself a good morning!

Security Blanket

Ever sat in the back of class to avoid being noticed? Or wildly over-prepared for a minor event? Or spent an entire party staring down at your phone instead of talking to people? These are called safety behaviors. They're little habits that can make you feel secure when you're stressed, like a blanket wrapped around you. They offer some short-term relief, but they don't really help you find the root of the problem. Getting too wrapped up in a security blanket can make it hard for you to move.

What are five safety behaviors you do?

1) ....

2) ....

3) ....

4) ....

5) ....

Now, circle one behavior that might not really be helping you. When you're next tempted to do that, what could you do instead?

....

....

....

....

....

....

....

....

....

....

Don't worry, you don't have to give it up forever!
It's okay if doing without your safety behavior feels weird at first.

Make Your Mantra

Anxiety is so freaking LOUD! Our minds are already filled with noise—a running list of thoughts—and when anxiety enters the picture, any room for quiet completely disappears. But coming up with your own personal mantra (a single word that makes you feel confident and capable whenever you need) can cut through the noise. In action movies, there's usually a scene where the hero's mentor gives them an inspiring pep talk to get past the final hurdle. Well, consider your mantra a personal rallying cry, and go into the world sure of yourself (and a little heroic too)!

Let's make that mantra!

What are five things you've done that you're proud of?

1) ....

2) ....

3) ....

4) ....

5) ....

Which of these achievements makes you feel the most confident?

....

....

....

....

....

Condense that achievement into one word.

....

Now that's a mantra! Say it whenever you need a boost!

Your thoughts are the architects of your destiny.

DAVID O. MCKAY

Anxiety on Trial

Don't you ever wish you could put your fears on trial? Well, lucky for you, you have a fear-specialist lawyer on hand who can argue your worries out of the room.

What's a bad thing that you often worry will happen?

....

....

....

Now, let your lawyer take a crack at it. What are three reasons it might not happen?

1) ....

2) ....

3) ....

Call a witness to the stand. Choose a wise person you know, or a famous person with good insight. Who are you calling?

....

What might your witness say about your fear?

....

....

Imagine your lawyer is giving you some argument advice. What would they say is the best way to fight your worries off?

....

....

....

Popcorn Please!

Whether it's on the couch or in theaters, movies are a great way to unwind and let your stresses disappear into the background.

Use the space below to make a watch list of comedies, tearjerkers, and action flicks to get your worries off your mind!

If you're a multitasker, color in this mandala while you watch a favorite film.
If not, color it in as you unpack that surprise ending. (Can you believe it???)

One day at a time
is all we do.
One day at a time
is good for you.

JOHN LENNON

Day by Day

Let's take it one day at a time.

What are some things that made you anxious today?

1) ....

2) ....

3) ....

What about them made you anxious?

....

....

....

....

Pick one of the items from your list. How can you ease your anxiety about it?

....

....

....

....

Once you do that, cross out the thing that made you anxious! How are you feeling now?

....

....

....

....

A Letter to Your Future Self

If you got a chance to talk to your future self, what would you want to know? In writing to a future version of yourself, you can think critically about who you are right now, and who you want to one day become. Use the following pages to write that letter. Keep in mind that delivery times vary—it might take a few years for your letter to reach the self you're writing to.

Focus on a future self at a specific time (e.g., in five or ten years) and consider the following questions:

- What hobbies does your future self enjoy?
- What does your future self do for work?
- Where does your future self live?
- Who does your future self spend time with?
- What things matter most to them?

Dear Self,

(continued)

Love,

You

The future cannot be predicted, but futures can be invented.

DENNIS GABOR

Consider the Odds

When faced with the unknown, we tend to expect the worst. A new mole, a clunk when you start the car, a giant bug disappearing into a crack in the wall (well, that one does evoke terror): You experience these things, and you're convinced something terrible will come to pass. There's a word for this: catastrophizing.

Catastrophizing involves two steps:

    1. Assuming something terrible will happen

    2. Assuming that when the terrible thing happens, you won't survive it

But before you spiral, ask yourself some leading questions, and ease your mind with probability.

What's something you're currently freaking out about?

What's the worst thing that could possibly happen?

What would need to be true for that to be possible?

What can you do if it happens?

Why might your prediction be false?

What's a more likely, more boring, outcome?

Now that you've answered those questions, color in the dice and remind yourself that the odds are in your favor.

Buoy Your Spirits

Lighthouses are incredible! Their constant light keeps ships afloat and on course during the darkest of nights and roughest of seas.

Let's get metaphorical. You're a ship, your anxiety is a stormy night threatening to tip you over, and the lighthouse is sending out reassuring messages that will guide you through the chaos.

Write three bright messages the lighthouse is beaming your way:

1) ....

....

....

2) ....

....

....

3) ....

....

....

Now keep those messages safe in your heart for the next storm,
and color this lighthouse in.

You're not you when you're anxious.

When the body is stressed, it's on high alert, responding to every situation as if it's life or death. This means that when you're anxious, you don't always behave or treat others the way you want to. But unless you're facing a wild bear, or pulling off a dangerous heist, your body can take a breather. So when a friend doesn't text you back, or your schedule gets derailed, remember: There's no crisis to avert! Before you respond with panic, try responding with love, and do something that makes your world a little brighter.

Fill out the columns with things that stress you out, how you typically respond in a panic, and loving actions you could take instead.

Stressful Thing	Panic Response	Loving Action

Best Possible Thing

All right, so you've got something coming up. It could be a job interview or a first date, but whatever it is, it's Stressing You Out! What if you spill coffee all over yourself? What if you find out you have a common ex? What if your ex is interviewing you, or your date is your boss?

Take a breath. Instead of jumping to the worst outcome, let's do the opposite, and sprint toward the best.

What's an event you have coming up?

....

....

....

....

What is the Best Possible Thing that could happen?

....

....

....

....

Tell us how great that would be!

....

....

....

....

Now that you're feeling a bit more confident, color in this mandala as you wait for your big moment.

Anti-Anxiety Amulet

An amulet is a charm designed to protect its wearer from harm. They're commonly made from gems, statues, drawings, plant and animal parts, and written words. But anything can be an amulet, as long as you believe in its power. So let's make some magic and build one!

What stresses would you like your amulet to protect you against?

....

....

Choose your container:

- ☐ Glass jar
- ☐ Leather pouch
- ☐ Silver capsule

Pick a flower:

- ☐ Lavender
- ☐ Orange blossom
- ☐ Goldenrod

Select something that shines:

- ☐ Sea glass
- ☐ Ruby
- ☐ Pearl

Where will you keep it?

- ☐ Around my neck
- ☐ On my wrist
- ☐ In my pocket

Now that you've crafted this amulet in your mind, it's time to put it on the page! Use the space below to draw your amulet and ward off any negative energy infringing on your peace.

Finish each day and be done with it.

RALPH WALDO EMERSON

Even what sucks will pass.

"No such thing as permanence" and "all things will pass" sound like stuff a gym teacher might say to you, usually when the class is running laps. But there's some truth in the clichés. It can feel like it takes forever, but eventually the things that burden you end up in the rearview.

What's one worry from your past that you've left behind in the dust?

_____

_____

_____

_____

_____

_____

What's one stressor you're facing now that you know is temporary?

_____

_____

_____

_____

_____

_____

_____

Happy Distractions

Sometimes when stress enters your life it's hard to think about anything else. But your life is bigger than your anxiety, and distractions can remind you of what's out there beyond your current fear. So list some happy diversions that absorb your attention, bring you joy, and give your stress the boot! Then fill the next page's field with flowers.

1) ....

....

....

2) ....

....

....

3) ....

....

....

4) ....

....

....

5) ....

....

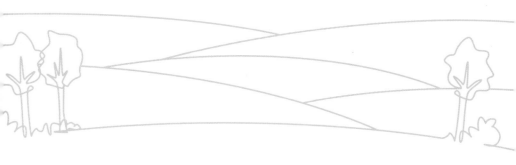

**When you awake in the morning,
think of what a precious privilege it is
to be alive, to think, to enjoy, to love.**

MARCUS AURELIUS

The "Nope" List

It can be hard to say no, especially when people act like they're owed your time. But when you've already got a lot on your plate, and someone you barely know asks you to help them move, the word "no" is crucial. So protect your time and say it with a smile. "No, thanks!"

Below, make a list of all the favors and time-wasters that you don't want to do anymore. When you stop doing each, be sure to cross it out with a big NOPE.

NOPE list:

Not gonna happen!

Maybe in the next life.

NOT MY JOB.

I'd like to say yes, but I love saying no.

Did hell freeze when you started talking?

❦Pop the Balloons!

Let loose your anxious thoughts! Put the things that are stressing you out inside these balloons, and visualize yourself popping them, or just letting them float away out of sight.

Some of us think holding on
makes us strong,
but sometimes it is letting go.

HERMANN HESSE

Five-Minute Brain Dump

Sometimes you just need to clear the thoughts clogging up your brain. A vent session with a friend can help, but when you don't have time to get brunch or talk on the phone, the Five-Minute Brain Dump is at your service. Use these pages to pour out everything on your mind. You can draw, you can write, you can even make charts and diagrams! Don't censor or edit yourself. Just be sure your brain is empty by the time you're done. And consider grabbing brunch anyway to treat yourself!

"If I don't think about this, it will definitely go away."

When dealing with anxiety, it's good to have a few reliable distractions that suspend panic. But sometimes our efforts to distract ourselves can, in the long run, add to our anxiety. Watching a funny TV show to decompress is good, but binge-watching it all night to avoid writing a final paper can hurt you.

Check off any of the following distractions that keep you from facing your anxieties, and feel free to add your own. Then in the opposite column, brainstorm ways you can prevent them from bringing you down.

- [ ] TV shows

....

....

....

- [ ] Video games

....

....

....

- [ ] Social media

....

....

....

- [ ] Texts from friends

....

....

....

- [ ] Chores

....

....

....

- [ ] News

....

....

....

....

....

....

....

....

....

....

Personal Peaceful Place

Think of a place that makes you happy. This could be a general location, like a forest or a beach, or more specific, like a favorite café or a friend's house. Visualizing it should bring you a sense of peace. Keep this place in your mind and answer the following questions. Then, whenever you're anxious, close your eyes and return there.

What is your peaceful place?

....

....

What do you like to do there?

....

....

....

What colors are in the scene?

....

....

What do you smell? What can you touch?

....

....

....

Find a small item that reminds you of your peaceful place, and keep it with you. What's the item?

....

....

In the space below, paste or draw things that remind you of your peaceful place. You can use newspaper clippings, magazine cutouts, photos, and more!

Confrontation Station

Sometimes people will hurt your feelings and cross your boundaries. You may have to confront them about it. Unfortunately, confrontation is the WORST! It's so stressful to face conflict head-on, even with people you really care about and trust. Often the most anxiety-inducing part is figuring out what to say. So fill in these prompts to create a script for talking about conflicts in your life. We've included a couple different scenarios, because confrontation is a common, if crappy, part of life.

Conflict: Someone has hurt you.

Describe what happened:

_____

_____

_____

_____

_____

How did it hurt you?

_____

_____

_____

_____

What do you need to feel at peace?

_____

_____

_____

_____

How can you invite the offending person to share their experience?

_____

_____

_____

_____

_____

Conflict: You need to set a boundary.

What boundary has been crossed?

....

....

....

....

How did it happen?

....

....

....

....

Why does that boundary need to be respected?

....

....

....

....

What steps are needed to enforce it?

....

....

....

....

Without courage…
we can't be kind,
true, merciful,
generous, or honest.

MAYA ANGELOU

Hall Pass

It can be hard to give ourselves permission to do the things we enjoy, especially if we're busy feeling guilty over other obligations. But everyone deserves a break! So fill out the following hall passes to give yourself the care you need. And wave your pass in the face of any monitor who dares to try and stop you!

Sometimes you just got to give yourself
what you wish someone else would give you.

PHILLIP C. MCGRAW

⁓Permission Slip

I give myself permission to: ....

I deserve this because: ....

Ways this will be great: ....

Date: ....

Signed: ....

⁓Permission Slip

I give myself permission to: ....

I deserve this because: ....

Ways this will be great: ....

Date: ....

Signed: ....

Permission Slip

I give myself permission to: ....

I deserve this because: ....

Ways this will be great: ....

Date: ....

Signed: ....

Permission Slip

I give myself permission to: ....

I deserve this because: ....

Ways this will be great: ....

Date: ....

Signed: ....

℘Permission Slip

I give myself permission to: ....

I deserve this because: ....

Ways this will be great: ....

Date: ....

Signed: ....

℘Permission Slip

I give myself permission to: ....

I deserve this because: ....

Ways this will be great: ....

Date: ....

Signed: ....

Power Washing Your Brain

Ever wish you could just pick up a hose and power wash away your negative thoughts?

Positive affirmations—pieces of uplifting self-talk—are like showers for your mind. Your brain acquires grime from the negative thoughts you carry. But affirmations that contradict those thoughts can clear away the gunk and leave you feeling better (and cleaner) than ever!

Come up with three affirmations (positive statements about yourself):

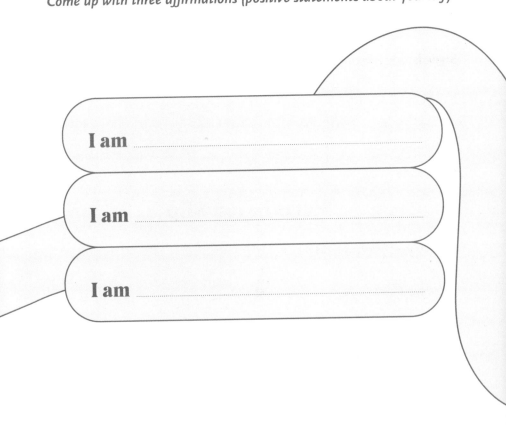

I am ....

I am ....

I am ....

Great start! But affirmations work best when you use them. So write your affirmations over and over in the spray from this hose. Don't stop until the page is overflowing!

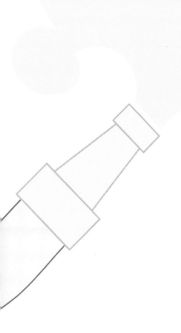

The Jar

Sure, it's not great to bottle up your emotions completely. But sometimes you're in a situation where you can't process your feelings right away. You may have other things on your plate, and need to move forward without being immobilized by stress. So put some of what's stressing you into the jar below, not to bottle up forever, but to open as soon as you have time and space for processing.

Now that you've closed the jar, spend some time centering yourself by coloring this mandala.

Nighttime Routine

Do you ever get into bed and find your mind suddenly overrun with anxieties, even if your day was relatively stress-free? When your head hits the pillow, all the problems simmering on the back burner hit a boiling point in your brain. But just like a good morning routine can set you up for success during the day, a good nighttime routine can get you to sweet dreams faster.

What are three tasks that stress you out in the morning?

1) ....

2) ....

3) ....

How can you prepare for each task before you go to sleep?

....

....

....

....

....

....

....

....

....

....

Now, check off the other things you can do to make your evening as calm as possible.

- ☐ Make a to-do list for the next day
- ☐ Journal your feelings before bed
- ☐ Cut out caffeine before dinner
- ☐ Play calming music
- ☐ Read a chapter of a novel
- ☐ Make time for skincare
- ☐ Practice meditation

5, 4, 3, 2, 1

Quick, don't think about it, just answer!

What are five things you can see?

1) ....

2) ....

3) ....

4) ....

5) ....

What are four things you can touch?

1) ....

2) ....

3) ....

4) ....

What are three things you can hear?

1) ....

2) ....

3) ....

What are two things you can taste?

1) ....

2) ....

What is one thing you can smell?

1) ....

The next time you start panicking, try this 5, 4, 3, 2, 1 exercise to ground yourself in the moment.

You were made for enjoyment, and the world was filled with things which you will enjoy.

JOHN RUSKIN

Wiki Article of You

It's easy to compare yourself to others: Olympic athletes who started sprinting at three, actors with more awards in their cabinets than you have mugs, your friend with the cool new job. It doesn't help that all that info is just a Wikipedia article (or group chat notification) away. But you've done cool things, too, and definitely changed a few others' lives for the better. So why not give yourself some attention? Write your own Wiki article full of the cool, interesting, funny, and noteworthy things in your life. It's not bragging if we ask ;).

Draw or paste in the top image of your Wiki article.

Early Life

Career

Philosophy

Influences

Special Projects

The River

Letting go is easier said than done. The things that hurt us and make us anxious have a strong hold. But our brains are powerful. We can affect our environment and our mental state through intentional thoughts and visualizations.

Take a deep breath, close your eyes, and picture the things that are hurting you. One by one, imagine dropping each of them into a calm river.

Find a blue colored pencil or marker. Use it to write words and phrases that remind you of your hurts in the river below. Then, color in the whole river with the same blue marker or pencil. Watch your hurts vanish beneath the blue water.

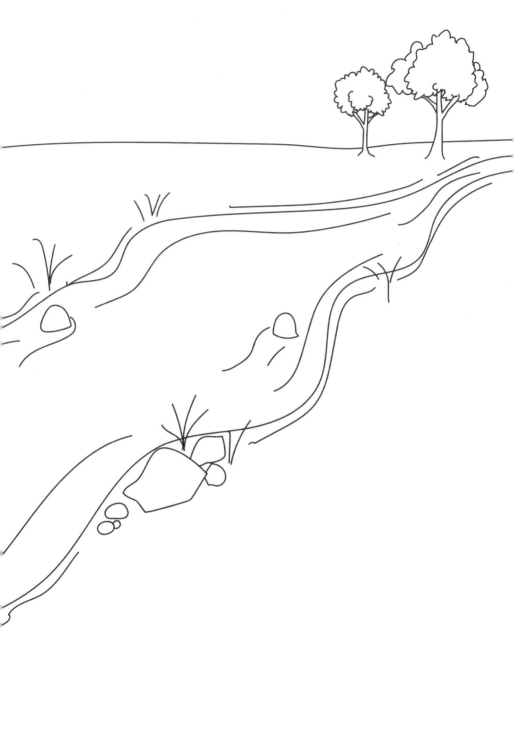

Mistakes Are Good, Actually

Screw-ups. Everyone, yes everyone, has them. Experts, celebrities, your parents —no one is free from the occasional mistake. Anxiety, however, doesn't like to let them go. If you try to move on, it puts you in a headlock like you're two wrestlers about to go pro.

But here's a truth that'll help you wriggle free and win the match: Screw-ups are actually awesome. Even if they don't give us funny stories for parties, they do something better. They give us the opportunity to grow.

What's one mistake you made a long time ago that taught you something useful?

How did you grow from it?

What's one recent mistake you're having trouble letting go of?

How can you wrestle free and learn from it?

Building a Safe Space

Home is for friends, for family, and most importantly, for you. Everyone deserves to feel comfortable and safe in their living space. Home should be a place where you can rest and recharge, where you can be your authentic self, and where you can reflect on your day's gifts and challenges. But it isn't always easy to achieve that. After all, it's not about interior design, it's about the objects and experiences that bring you peace. Consider the following questions and see if you can bring the answers into your home.

When I take the time to take care of myself ... I feel like I can face life with a renewed vigor and renewed passion.

VIOLA DAVIS

What's an object that makes you comfortable?

What is your favorite song?

What is your favorite book?

What colors bring you joy?

What textures do you like?

What tastes do you enjoy?

New Perspectives

Anxiety can make a single event seem like the most important, catastrophic thing ever to happen. But just because something feels like the end of the world, doesn't mean that it is. The stories we tell can shape our reality, but the stories you tell about yourself don't necessarily match the stories other people have to share. Everyone has embarrassing or stressful moments. But if you take a step back, you won't just gain clarity on those moments, you might even find something to laugh at too.

Change the way you look at things and the things you look at change.

WAYNE DYER

What's an event that stressed you out recently?

Now, zoom out. Tell the story from a different point of view.

What are some differences between these two stories?

What's something about that event you can laugh at?

One good thing about music, when it hits you, you feel no pain.

BOB MARLEY

Whatever! Playlist

Sometimes, you've just gotta get on the road, crank up the tunes, and leave behind the things that have been bothering you.

Use the space below to make a playlist for whenever you need to clear your head.

Song title   **Artist**

Ghosting

Yes, ghosting is mean. But if you've ever used a dating app, you know it can be necessary. If someone makes you doubt yourself, or feel like you can't try new hobbies, or that you don't deserve to do the things you enjoy, that's not the kind of energy you need. You've got our full permission to ghost them. And you know what really needs to be ghosted? Your anxiety. It's not letting you have a good time! And isn't that what we're all on this big round ball to do?

So make a list of five messages your anxiety sends you that simply do not deserve a response, and ghost away!

1) ....

....

2) ....

....

3) ....

....

4) ....

....

5) ....

....

Anxiety really *is* like a bad date. What would its dating profile look like? Imagine it, and then swipe left.

Anxiety's Dating Profile

I like to

....

....

....

....

My ideal weekend includes

....

....

....

....

When we're together, you can expect

....

....

....

....

By the way, I never

....

....

....

....

Move On and Move Out

From a bad roommate who never does the dishes, to memories of teasing at school, unfairness can eat away at you. You can't always move out immediately, or protect your younger self from unkindness. However, instead of fixating on your roommate's messes, or wishing your past had been better, you can work to accept the things you can't change, and enjoy the present moment as best you can.

What's something unfair that's been bothering you?

....

....

....

....

Give yourself a break! Finish this sentence:

It makes sense that this bothers me because . . .

....

....

....

....

What are three things you can do to distract yourself and enjoy the here and now?

1) ....

2) ....

3) ....

Self-Care Rituals

Having an activity that centers you is crucial. Think of yourself like a bathtub, and anxiety like running water. When you have anxiety, it's like the bathtub is always almost full, which means whenever the faucet turns on, you start to panic. A calming ritual opens the drain. It lowers the amount of water in the tub, so when new stressors pour into your life, you're able to process them without overflowing.

The greatest thing in the world is to know how to belong to oneself.

MICHEL DE MONTAIGNE

What's one calming activity you can do?

....

....

How often can you commit to doing it?

....

....

....

Tell us how it went!

....

....

....

....

....

....

....

....

....

....

....

....

....

....

Write a Letter to Your Past Self

Who were you five years ago? Or ten? What would you say if you could talk to the person you were then with the information and experience you have now? On the following page, write a letter to yourself from the past with some of the wisdom you've learned over the years.

Some tips to get started:

- Try to go back at least five years.
- Look back to moments of transition (the first day of college, before you started a new job, etc.).

For advice, consider the following:

- What should your past self look out for?
- What have you learned in the years after?
- Who should you spend time with?
- What hobbies should you pursue?
- What things are most important?

Don't forget to be nice! This is you, after all.

Dear past _____,

(continued)

Love,

Your Future Self

> You, too, are your past; often your face
> is your autobiography.

WILL DURANT

Freedom from Restriction

Stop! Do you have any restrictive rules for yourself (like never eating after 7:00, or only drinking coffee twice a week)? General guidelines can give your life structure, but sometimes, you gotta let yourself have fun!

What are three rules you have for yourself?

1) ....

2) ....

3) ....

Why do you have these rules? Do they ever get in the way of living your life?

....

....

....

....

....

Pick one you're willing to bend on (even if it's just a little). How are you going to treat yourself?

....

....

....

....

....

Now, enjoy that iced coffee (or whatever you picked!) and remember that most rules aren't written in stone for a reason.

As you're treating yourself, color in this mandala!

Inner Sanctum

Does the phrase "inner sanctum" bring to mind a superhero's secret lair, or a wizard's tower? You can have your own inner sanctum, and bring it everywhere you go: a secret home base for personal contemplation. Every time you take a quiet moment to consider important questions about your life, you step into your inner sanctum. But when you're stressed, the mental noise can make your sanctum difficult to access. Crafting a mental image of this contemplative place will help you enter it whenever you need to.

Take a few deep breaths and imagine a calm room. What colors do you notice?

....

....

....

What items do you see in the room?

....

....

....

What sounds populate the room?

....

....

....

Now, imagine a small box in the room's center that can hold all of your important concerns. What questions will you place in the box?

....

....

....

....

....

Congratulations, you have now crafted an inner sanctum of your own, which you can access whenever the need arises. Lucky you!

The Freakout Flu

Anxiety starts in your brain, but like that guy who takes up three seats on the bus, it sprawls all over the place.

When you're anxious, your nervous system may go into fight-or-flight mode. It doesn't care that you can't punch your upcoming exam in the face or dash away from an awkward social situation like an Olympic sprinter. It thinks you need to deal with a physical threat, and gets your body pumped to do that. Which would be cool if you needed to outrun a tiger, but normally just makes you feel like crap.

Where does anxiety show up in your body? Does it tense your shoulders, crank up your heartbeat, make your hands sweat, upset your stomach, cause chills, give you weird aches? On the next page, color or draw where anxiety hits you hardest physically. Understanding your physical anxiety symptoms can keep them from adding to your stress.

Visualize the stress flowing out of your physical anxiety hot spots. Some people find meditation techniques like progressive relaxation helpful; if that sounds like your jam, try looking up guided meditations online.

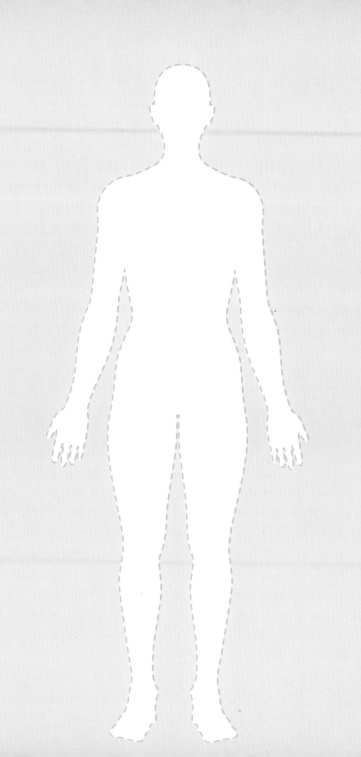

Outfit to Uplift

While confidence does come from within, it doesn't hurt to boost it from the outside.

What's an outfit that makes you feel on top of the world?

....

....

....

....

....

What about it makes you feel confident?

....

....

....

....

....

What are some events you have coming up that might require the confidence boost?

....

....

....

....

....

....

> I consider it a compliment that I am full of myself. . . . I am not afraid of honoring myself.
>
> OPRAH WINFREY

Negative Thought Fighter

See that buff dude below? Consider him your Negative Thought Bodyguard™. Anytime you think something bad about yourself, he jumps in and kicks (or punches) it away. No nasty thought is getting anywhere near you with him around.

Fill in the thought bubbles with some unkind beliefs you've had about yourself, and let your bodyguard handle it.

Say you're talking to your bodyguard about self-defense. What advice would he give you for defending yourself against those intrusive beliefs?

Portrait of the Inner Critic

Who is that needling voice in your head giving you a hard time? It never gives you a break. It's basically the micromanager of your life, finding fault in everything you do and looking to make you feel small. This voice is so omnipresent, it can almost feel like it's your own. But if you can separate yourself from your inner critic, you'll be better equipped to stand up to it.

Give your inner critic a name:

....

When do they like to bother you most?

1) ....

2) ....

3) ....

How can you tell them to BACK OFF?

....

....

....

....

....

....

....

....

Now that you've given this jerk a name, time to give them a face! Draw your inner critic below, and when you're done, tell them to get lost!

Confidence Armor

Sticks and stones may break your bones, but weird comments can mess with your head. Do you ever wish you had a shield to protect you from other people's judgments? Well, you do! Like a superhero with sci-fi armor, your strengths and the things that bring you joy protect you from even the most passive-aggressive crap.

Design your Confidence Coat of Arms. In each of the shield's four parts, draw something that represents you. This can be a hobby, a value, or a role you play in your community. Give the shield a name in the banner below it!

Find out who you are and be that person.

ELLEN DEGENERES

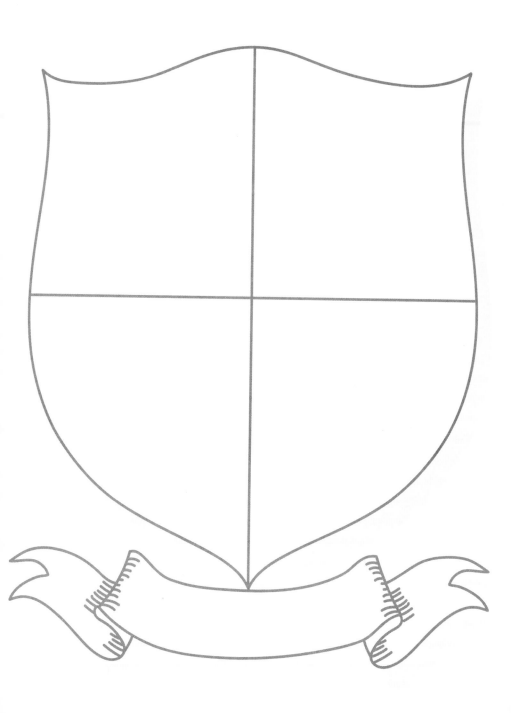

Inner Strengths

The anxious brain loves to focus on mistakes. It's the epitome of a micromanager; it constantly checks up on you to make sure you're doing everything right, and if a single thing isn't up to par, it lets you have it. That barrage of negativity can obscure your strengths (yes, you are pretty dang strong!), and worse, can make you feel like it's not worth trying to improve at all.

Put your anxious brain in the corner for a minute, and check off the boxes on the opposite page to take credit for your strengths.

Self-love . . . is not so vile a sin as self-neglecting.

WILLIAM SHAKESPEARE

- [ ] I am funny
- [ ] I am considerate
- [ ] I am a hard worker
- [ ] I am thoughtful
- [ ] I am loving
- [ ] I am generous
- [ ] I am courageous
- [ ] I am open-minded
- [ ] I am curious
- [ ] I am creative
- [ ] I am fair
- [ ] I am hopeful
- [ ] I am appreciative
- [ ] I am a leader
- [ ] I am authentic
- [ ] I am brave
- [ ] I am spontaneous
- [ ] I am in touch with my emotions
- [ ] I know myself
- [ ] I am trusting
- [ ] I am steadfast
- [ ] I am humble
- [ ] I am organized
- [ ] I learn from my mistakes

Choose one of the strengths you checked off on the previous page. What have you done recently that embodies that strength?

....

....

....

....

How can you share that strength with others?

....

....

....

....

....

....

....

....

....

....

....

....

....

....

Choose one strength that you didn't check off. Why don't you feel like you possess that quality?

What can you do to develop that strength?

What's one thing you can do right now (yes, this very second!) to try it out?

Compassion Fashion

We all have traits we don't like. It can be very easy to be selfish, like when there's one slice of pizza left at a party and you missed lunch, or irritable, like when you snap at a friend after a rough day. It feels embarrassing to act in a way that's not consistent with your values. But shoving those traits away and pretending they don't exist is unkind to the person who needs kindness most—you! So be honest and face the moments when you weren't your best. Then show yourself some compassion.

I was a little selfish when . . .

I can forgive myself because . . .

Sometimes I'm mean by . . .

But I try to be kind through . . .

I don't like it when I . . .

I can change that through . . .

_____

_____

_____

_____

_____

_____

_____

_____

_____

_____

_____

_____

_____

> Love yourself the way you would love your friend . . . taking care of yourself, nourishing yourself, trying to understand, comfort, and strengthen yourself.
>
> FREDERICK BUECHNER

Inner Mentor

Now that you've told your inner critic to get lost (if you haven't, go back a few pages!), it's time to bring a more helpful voice into the conversation. While a critic can be harsh and demeaning, a mentor is concerned most of all with guiding their mentee. When you make mistakes, your inner mentor will give you compassionate direction, and when you succeed, your inner mentor will cheer you on.

What's a mistake you made recently?

....

....

....

What constructive feedback would your mentor give you?

....

....

....

What's a recent accomplishment of yours?

....

....

....

How would your mentor congratulate you? How have you worked hard for this?

....

....

....

....

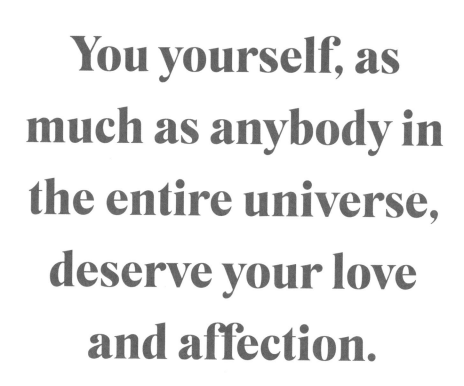

You yourself, as much as anybody in the entire universe, deserve your love and affection.

SHARON SALZBERG

Imperfection Selection

It's normal to aim for perfection, to want perfect relationships, jobs, even a perfect world! But trying to be perfect is exhausting, and it invokes tons of anxiety because no matter how hard you try, or how well you plan with your bullet journal, perfection is unattainable. In learning not only to accept but to love the parts of yourself and your life that are imperfect, you can lose the stress and enjoy all things asymmetrical, misshapen, and wonderful.

What are some things you love, not in spite of but because of their imperfections?

1) ....

....

2) ....

....

3) ....

....

4) ....

....

5) ....

....

Now, color in this imperfect produce and remember that the shape of a carrot doesn't determine how good it tastes with a little olive oil and thyme, baked at 350 degrees for fifteen minutes.

Sounds of, Well, Not Silence

Time to drown out some of the racket inside your head with the better chatter outside of it. Let's make some noise!

What are the sounds of your favorite restaurant?

....

....

....

....

What are the sounds of a good party?

....

....

....

....

Describe the best laugh you've ever heard.

....

....

....

....

What sounds do you associate with peace?

....

....

....

....

What do you remember from your favorite concert?

....

....

....

....

What sounds remind you of home?

....

....

....

....

> **Music expresses that which cannot be said and on which it is impossible to be silent.**
>
> VICTOR HUGO

Your Great Traits

Don't let anybody, especially yourself, convince you that you're not great! Below, write about the times you've displayed each of the following qualities. If your brain is trying to tell you that you're not good enough, look back on these and remember, you're a freaking wonderful person!

Courage

....

....

....

Kindness

....

....

....

Responsibility

....

....

....

Love

....

....

....

Generosity

....

....

Wisdom

Humor

Determination

Resilience

Creativity

Believe you can
and you're halfway there.

THEODORE ROOSEVELT

The Art of Reframing

When people say "good vibes only," it's like, okay, but how? When anxiety barrages you with its "what if you're not good enough?" spiel, thinking positively doesn't always cut it. You've gotta tackle those negative thoughts head-on. That's why reframing can be a great tool. If your anxiety says, "I'm not smart," responding "I'm actually a genius" probably won't convince you or make you feel better. Instead, shine a new light on that negative thought by reframing it as: "I'm aware of my mistakes." You don't have to deny your feelings, but reframing lets you give them nuance.

Give it a try! What are five negative beliefs you have about yourself?

1) ....

....

2) ....

....

3) ....

....

4) ....

....

5) ....

....

Now put these beliefs into new frames! Write a reframed, compassionate version of each negative thought in the picture frames.

Inkblot Analysis

Anxiety doesn't want you to trust your own judgment. It needles you with questions until you're insecure in your opinions. But who is anxiety to say that your point of view is wrong? It can't see the future! By trusting yourself, you can solve problems creatively, considering paths and opportunities that you might have been closed off to before.

So let's get inspired! Look at the inkblots on the following pages, and tell us what they are and what they mean. There are no wrong answers here, so believe in your interpretations and start imagining.

Make a list of five things you see in this inkblot:

1) ....

....

2) ....

....

3) ....

....

4) ....

....

5) ....

Turn the page upside down and look again. Do you see anything new?

....

....

....

....

....

....

....

....

Take one minute to describe what you see in this inkblot:

....

....

....

....

Now, tell a story. How did the figure(s) come to exist? What situation appears in the ink? What emotions do you see?

....

....

....

....

....

....

....

....

....

....

....

....

....

....

....

Secret Kindness

Did you know? You're a really nice person! And because you're nice, you probably don't like to brag about it. But even if you're not going to tell others, you should still admit it to yourself! Answer the following questions and know a little self-praise never hurt anybody.

How do you believe others should be treated?

....

....

....

....

....

....

....

....

How do you live in accordance with those values?

....

....

....

....

....

....

....

....

....

What's a small kindness you consistently practice?

What's the most generous thing you've ever done?

On that best portion of a good man's life,
His little, nameless, unremembered acts
Of kindness and of love.

WILLIAM WORDSWORTH

Award Season

You've come a long way! While this trophy might not go up on a shelf in your bedroom, you deserve it nonetheless. So tell us what you did, and then design an award worthy of the accomplishment!

What are you receiving this trophy for?

How long have you been working toward this accomplishment?

Use the rest of this page to write your "thank you" speech!

Decorate the trophy with stuff related to your accomplishment, and write your name on it!

Hand Me Over!

All right, time to step away! Really. Believing in yourself is hard work, especially if you're anxious about how others see you, so call a friend and pass these pages to them.

If you're still reading, stop! These questions are for your friend to answer only!

Is the owner of this journal gone? Good. You have a very important job. Answer the following questions and let your friend know how loved they are! (Don't flip through the rest of the journal; it's personal, and only these pages are for your eyes.)

My friend's best qualities are . . .

Something I really admire about them is . . .

My best memory of my friend is . . .

If I could give them one piece of advice, it would be . . .

Those who bring sunshine into the lives of others cannot keep it from themselves.

J. M. BARRIE

Quotes of Confidence

Ever hear something that resonates with you so deeply that you wish you could write it down? Well, here's the space for that compilation! Write down all the quotes that make you feel capable as heck. And be sure to keep them with you long after you close this book.